Contents

Foreword: Your Mission 05

Part One:
Let Go to Live Big

A Story of Living Bigger 08

The Signposts of Living Small 09

How Boldness Leads to Bliss 10

Part Two:
Learn to Live Bigger

The Method 12

The Model 13

Part Three:
The 6 Live Bigger Practices

READINESS 16

Advice Articles

> Embrace Fear 19

> Don't Let Perfection Stunt
  Your Bliss 21

> 4 Tips for Wrangling
  Procrastination 23

> Live on Your Own Terms 25

Leading Question 27

CAPACITY 29

Advice Articles

> Start a Rejuvenation Program 33

> That Nagging Feeling:
  'I want to do more with my life' 35

> Life: How Much Can
  You Handle? 37

> Stop Pushing Yourself
  to the Brink 38

Leading Question 39

WORTHINESS 41

Advice Articles

> Get to Know Your Worthiness 45

> How Joy Unveiled My
  Dark Little Secret 47

> The Irony of Worthiness 49

> A Lesson from Oprah 51

Leading Question 53

VALUES 55

Advice Articles

> The Emptiness of Goals
  Without Values 57

> Change the Game 58

> Find Your Core Values 59

> Gut Check: Are You Being
  the Real You? 61

Leading Question 63

BOUNDARIES 65

Advice Articles

> Whose Boundaries Are
  You Crossing? 67

> Avoiding Rage at Home
  and Work 69

> You Need Boundaries Too 71

> I Broke My Own Rule 73

Leading Question 75

PURPOSE 77

Advice Articles

> 3 Revealing Questions 79

> Find Your Purpose 81

> Your Purpose Is What
  You Deem It to Be 82

> Living Your Purpose 83

Leading Question 85

Part Four:
Advice for Your Journey

Boldness Essentials 88

Don't Just Read it, Live it 90

Afterword 91

Acknowledgments 92

About the Author 93

Foreword: Your Mission

What's stopping you from living a big, bold, glorious life?

Ah yes. I mean even bigger and bolder than the life you have right now. I'm talking about the kind of life that you can look back on 40 years from now and think, 'Wow. I don't know how I did all that, but what an extraordinary ride.'

Your mission, if you are willing to accept it, is to get out of your own way. Let go of all those niggling, annoying, life-stalling things between you and your boldest dreams.

To do this, you'll need to become an explorer, bravely journeying inward. You'll need to uncover your self-beliefs, stare them dead in the eye and eradicate anything that's bogging you down.

Simple concept, right? But it will take courage and chutzpa to get from where you are today to where you want to be.

I've created this guide to assist you on your quest. It features 6 practices specifically designed to help you go from playing small to living big. These practices have worked for me and thousands of people I've coached over the past 15 years.

Know this: you can create a bigger life.

It all begins with letting go.

Be bold,

Lisa

Lisa Martin, PCC

Part One:

LET GO TO LIVE BIG

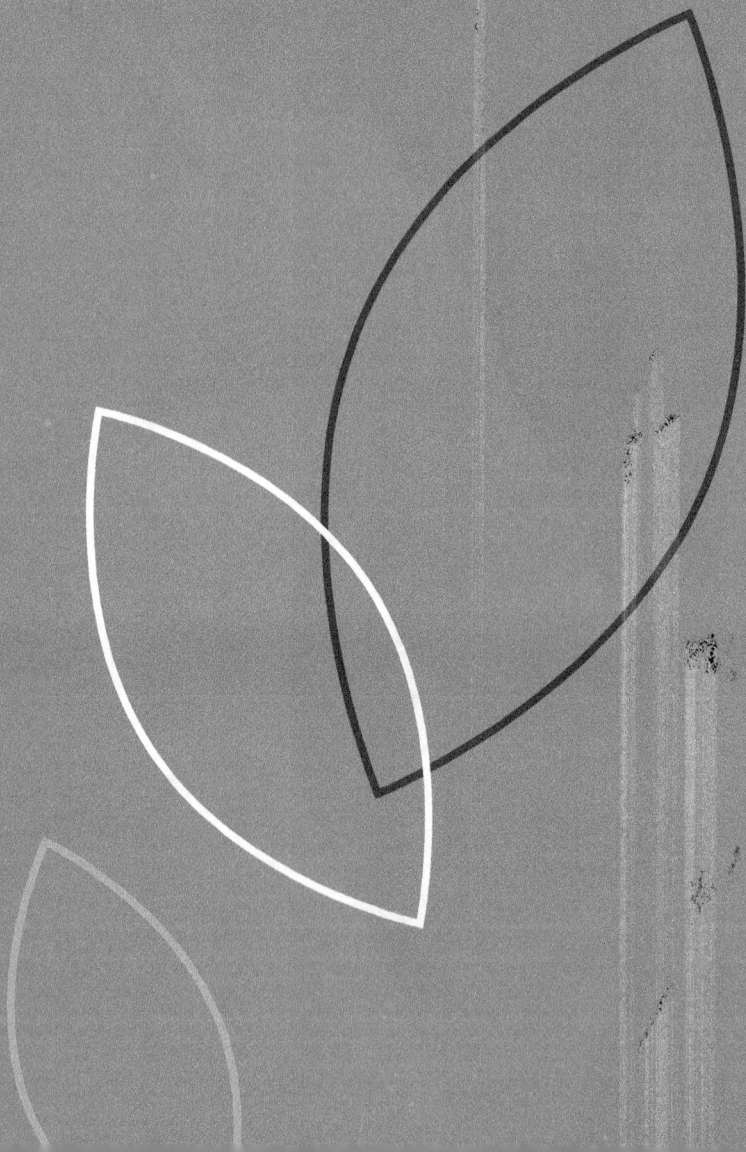

A Story of Living Bigger

When I met Cassie several years ago at a conference, I was struck by her smarts.

Here was a 41-year old woman with an exciting media career, and a million fascinating projects on the go. She'd been married for 15 years and had two kids under 10.

To the naked eye, she exuded success. But as we talked, I began to see beneath the surface.

Cassie had a subtle unease about her. Despite working herself to the bone and creating a full, busy life, she felt incomplete. Underachieved. Dissatisfied. She described it as a nagging, incessant feeling that she was supposed to be doing more.

I identified two things in Cassie as we chatted. First, she was on the fast train to burnout and her end-point would not be pretty. Second, she needed to crank up her courage so she could make different decisions about her life.

I began coaching her. Our work together focused on identifying and attacking the nasty, life-limiting beliefs lurking in her mind.

Together, we uncovered Cassie's secret belief that she needed to contain her aspirations to avoid disappointment. We also learned she always stuck with 'safe' career choices endorsed by family and friends rather than listening to her gut.

With these realizations, her journey to live bigger began.

Within a year, she made a bold leap to a newly created position at her company. The job was directly aligned with her passion for community relations. It allowed her to work from home two days a week, freeing up more time for family and volunteer work at an animal shelter.

This triggered the release valve on her stress. She was a woman renewed. She certainly wasn't less busy, but she was significantly more fulfilled.

Living bigger isn't necessarily about having the world's most audacious aspirations. It's about daring to make the choices you really want to make as a leader and in life.

The Signposts
of Living Small

People often have no idea they're living small.

You can have a stellar job, wonderful family and the prettiest home on the block. But you're still living small if your life choices don't match your deepest, truest, boldest desires.

The decision to live small happens beneath the surface. Consciously you believe you're doing exactly what you want. In reality there are silent, self-sabotaging thoughts steering your destiny. These thoughts lead you to be less than your true potential and to have less than you really want.

Here are 7 living small signposts to watch for:

1 Do you envy other people?

2 Do you compare yourself to others?

3 Are you regretful?

4 Are you dissatisfied?

5 Do you often wish for things but fail to take action to get them?

6 Have you settled for 'good enough?'

7 Do you believe you don't deserve much more than what you already have?

If any of these signposts sound like you, there's a good chance you're living a smaller life than you desire.

How Boldness Leads to Bliss

Living your biggest life doesn't happen by accident. It happens when you decide go for more than what's within easy reach.

It's about bravely exploring inward, acknowledging your desires and pushing past the internal nonsense that tells you 'no.'

As simple and frustrating as it may be, your biggest roadblocks to a fuller, richer life are inside your head and, possibly, your heart.

To arrive at bliss, you need to boldly ...

1 Stop blaming yourself and others for your circumstances.

2 Acknowledge what you really want in life.

3 Search for hidden beliefs that stop you from having what you want.

4 Destroy those limiting beliefs.

5 Create empowering, life-changing beliefs about yourself.

Your path to living big will have obstacles. You will be tested. You will have to take brave leaps.

Also be prepared that discomfort is just part of the journey, so brace yourself. Evolution doesn't happen without discomfort so learn to embrace it. Trust me, comfort won't lead you anywhere new. That's why boldness is essential.

Part Two:

LEARN
TO LIVE
BIGGER

The Method

The Live Bigger Practices can be applied by anyone, regardless of their current circumstances.

The structure of this book is based on a self-coaching model to help you develop greater self-awareness and use the Live Bigger Practices in your everyday work and life.

In this book you will find:

1 The **Live Bigger Model,** featuring the 6 practices to create the life you want.

2 **An explanation of each Live Bigger Practice** and why it matters.

3 **Four Advice Articles for each Live Bigger Practice** to deepen your understanding.

4 **One Leading Question for each Live Bigger Practice** to help you gain self-awareness.

5 **(Optional) Live Bigger Assessment.**

The Model

Let me introduce you to the **Live Bigger Model.**

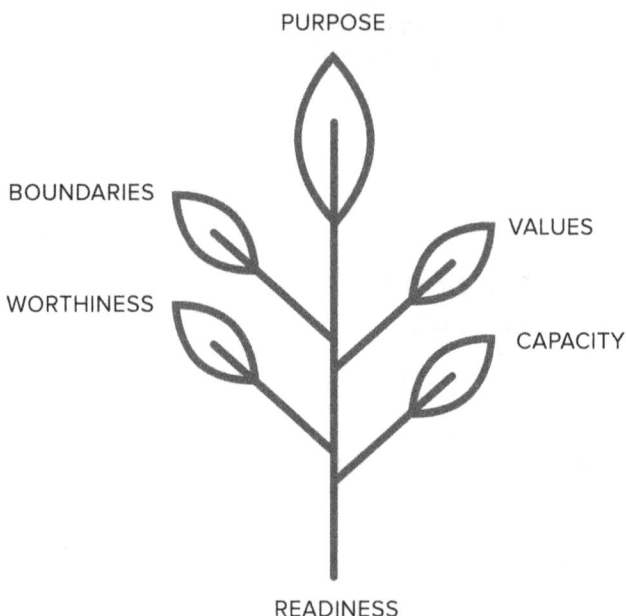

PURPOSE

BOUNDARIES

VALUES

WORTHINESS

CAPACITY

READINESS

I created this model based on my work as a leadership coach over the past 15 years. During this time, I've helped thousands of people live bigger lives by shattering limiting beliefs and charting new, bolder paths for themselves.

Along the way, I've delivered hundreds of workshops, conducted in-depth interviews and learned exactly what it takes to get where you want in life ... and what will stop you in your tracks.

The Live Bigger Model is also informed by my personal journey. I was an accomplished but unfullfilled corporate executive who took a huge leap, recreating my entire life to find my true happiness.

Without further ado, here are the 6 Practices to Live Bigger:

1 **Readiness:** See what's preventing you from living a bigger life.

2 **Capacity:** Manage stress and demands.

3 **Worthiness:** Love who you are.

4 **Values:** Know what matters most to you and live up to it.

5 **Boundaries:** Create harmony by setting clear limits for yourself and others.

6 **Purpose:** Decide what you're meant to do on this planet.

The 6 practices featured in this guide must be experienced as a set, which is to say you can't select just a few and find your way to living big.

The practices build on each other, and work in tandem. So make sure you don't take shortcuts or underestimate the importance of each one.

This is key to living big.

Part Three:

THE 6 PRACTICES TO LIVE BIGGER

Readiness

Take heed. You might be in massive resistance and not even know it. And if you are, your **readiness** will be very low.

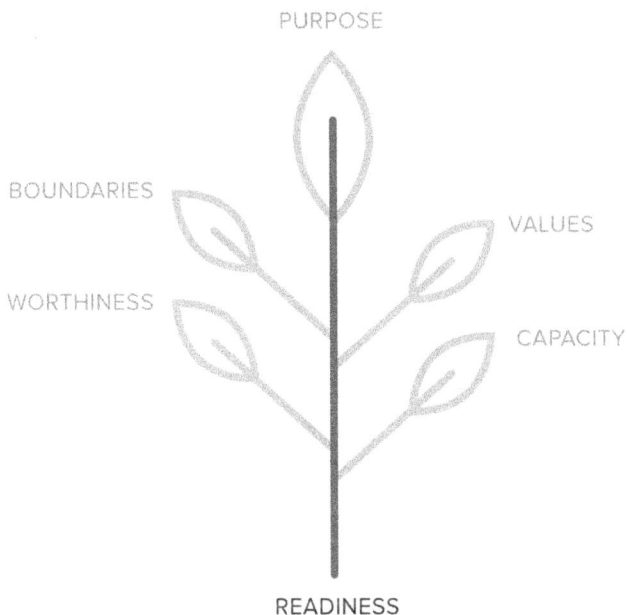

PURPOSE

BOUNDARIES

VALUES

WORTHINESS

CAPACITY

READINESS

Readiness is your willingness and capacity to take on change and engage in activities that will lead to your bliss.

Resistance is the opposite of **readiness.**

Resistance is a bliss buster. It can be invisible to the naked eye but fog up your ability to envision the life you really want. It will make you stall on the bold, brave life changes you sincerely want to make.

Resistance is rooted in fear ... fear that you'll make the wrong choice, get hurt, be disappointed or let someone down.

So, are you ready to change?

Start by noticing your patterns of resistance and intervene (gently) in your own behavior. Ask yourself to behave differently than your norm.

Take an action that contradicts your typical behavior. That new action will shake up your thought patterns. Inspiration will follow, resulting in more bold actions. Before you know it, major life change is unfolding.

A Chinese proverb says, 'Inspiration does not beget action. Action begets inspiration.' I urge you to really hear this. This ancient truth tells you how to begin living bigger.

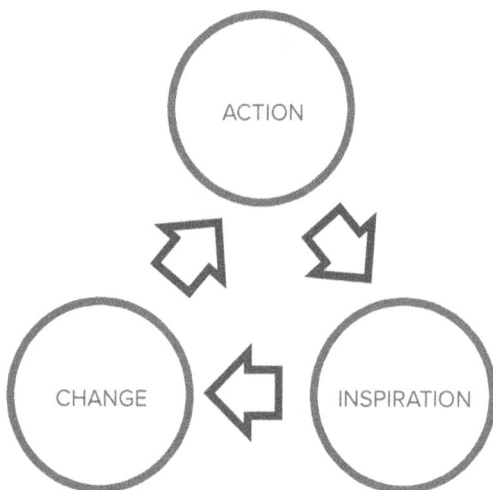

ACTION

INSPIRATION

CHANGE

What I'm saying is this: Living a bigger, bolder life starts with a **readiness** to take action. Don't wait for inspiration to drop from the sky. Just begin. **Act. Move forward.**

You won't uncover resistance in yourself unless you're hunting for it. So here are 3 major alarm bells to watch for:

1 **Perfectionism**. Perfectionists spin their wheels waiting for ideal timing and circumstances, afraid of jumping too soon. They grip tightly to their way of doing things, not accepting help or taking chances that could move them forward.

If you're a perfectionist, you may see it as a lovely trait. Rethink this urgently. It's resistance dressed up in a well-tailored suit. It messes with your head and will stop you from living a bigger, fuller life.

2 **Procrastination**. Do you delay actions that could change your life? Stall tactics are energy-snatchers. They leave you depleted and disappointed that you keep ending up in the same place.

If you're a procrastinator, you often think you're too busy to make major change right now. This is because you're masterful at prioritizing other tasks above those that actually lead to what you want. This is rooted in fear of change and the unknown.

3 **Pain Avoidance**. This one's a doozy. Fear of emotional pain can be an invisible wall between you and what you most want. It's choosing not to choose because you might fail, be rejected or heart-broken.

Yes of course, it's natural to have fears. And yes, the bolder you are, the more likely you will experience failure, rejection and heartbreak now and then.

Here's the crux of the issue though. Would you rather look back on a big, rich, textured life where you dared to go after your strongest desires? Or a safe, even-keeled life with few risks and muted happiness? Either choice is valid, but make it consciously.

Embrace Fear

Here's an interesting note on human nature. People tend to stay the same unless they believe they have more to gain than lose by changing.

That's why people stay in unhealthy relationships or careers they find unsatisfying. It's why some people are always cooking up a grand new scheme, but never actually implement it.

More often than not, people give into fears far too easily, worried about what they might lose by going in a new direction. Fear plays on the mind, occupying space.

It's wise to actively evaluate your choices based on the questions: 'What have I got to lose?' and 'What have I got to gain?' You're likely to make bolder, braver decisions because this forces you to give airtime to the positive side of the equation.

Make sure you note how all of your possible gains become losses if you don't pursue the change.

Case in point: Let's say you have a secret, untapped passion for art. Do you make room in your frantic life for an art class once a week? Your mind instantly populates with downsides: you'll have less free time, there might be homework, you might hate the class, you might be the worst student ... on and on.

But what might you gain? You might open up new channels of creativity. Art might become an integral part of your life. You might meet fascinating people. You might feel energized.

The way you handle this kind of decision is indicative of how you live your life. Do you forsake major possible gains to give into minor fears?

If so, start letting yourself take smart risks more often. Eventually, through trial and error, you'll gain crucial self-awareness, allowing you to design a life you love. And you'll collect some intriguing anecdotes along the way.

"Our lives improve
only when we take
chances – and
the first and most
difficult risk we can
take is to be honest
with ourselves."

Walter Anderson

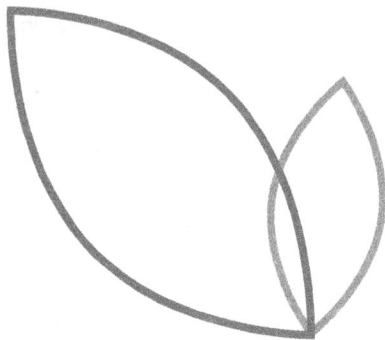

Don't Let Perfection Stunt Your Bliss

Perfection will kill your happiness.

When you focus on making everything 'perfect,' you inevitably get stuck. You hold on too tightly. Pride interferes with admitting you need help.

Perfection sucks up energy you could otherwise invest in trying new things and getting creative with your life.

A few years ago I had a client — let's call her Caroline — who was near breakdown. Her misery was evident to everyone around her.

At work, she never missed a deadline but she drove her team insane with micromanagement, never giving people a chance to do things their own way.

Her home was a mausoleum, not a speck of dust in sight. She discussed at length how only she could clean it 'properly' — her husband and kids were incapable. No professional was up to the task.

Caroline required an intervention. I gently worked with her to realize the stone-cold truth: perfectionism was destroying her. She'd lost grip on reality and any sense of joy she once had.

What perfectionists can't see is that perfection controls them, but it gives them the twisted notion that they're the ones in control.

With time and some concerted work, Caroline loosened her grip and found her way back to a balanced way of being.

Let her story be a cautionary tale. Get real with yourself: You can't control everything. If you want to grow and change, you'll need to relinquish some control. You'll need to wander into unknown territory.

The sooner you set yourself free from perfectionism, the sooner you can find bigger, deeper happiness.

Here are 4 steps to take now:

1 **Redefine success.** Realistically, no one and nothing is perfect. No career is perfect and no life is perfect. Create a new definition for success that removes perfection from the equation. Replace it with the love of progress, learning and growth.

2 **Learn to let go.** Eliminate your desire to be master of the universe. Acknowledge you could use some support. Then, get comfortable asking for help and collaborating with others. This will ease your load and allow you to look ahead for opportunities rather than being mired in the here and now.

3 **Challenge yourself.** The only way you'll know if you can complete a triathlon, give a speech, have a tough conversation or get a promotion is if you take the leap. Stop worrying about a future you cannot predict. Stop telling yourself you're not ready to jump. If you feel 80 percent ready, it's time to take on the challenge. Let yourself love the experience of going after what you want even if you don't succeed every time.

4 **Aim for progress.** The truth is, perfectionism often keeps its practitioners so busy, they rarely have time to seek or experience their bliss. If you aim for progress instead of perfection, you will have more time to actually enjoy life.

4 Tips for Wrangling Procrastination

Oh I know how strong your intent can be to start or complete a project and yet, there it is: procrastination.

It's a problem as old as time itself, but don't let yourself believe it's not solvable. The thing about procrastination is you need to grab it by the throat and wrangle it in. And these specific tips will help you do just that.

4 ways to to get things done:

1 **Find your kick-start comfort zone.** For many procrastinators, the very first steps of a new project are the hardest. Once they get going, all is well. I believe everyone has certain things that can ease their discomfort at this initial stage. Maybe you need to grab a latte at your favorite coffee shop and spend an hour completing your initial step.

2 **Reward yourself for progress.** I mean this literally. Call a friend for a chat, treat yourself to some chocolate, take a walk in nature ... whatever floats your boat. If you celebrate progress along the way, you're more likely to keep moving forward.

3 **Stop berating yourself when you stall.** You're human. Accept imperfection. Yes, you may find yourself procrastinating again. Congratulate yourself for noticing! Then move on.

4 **Focus on one step at a time.** Even small steps are awesome steps. Some days you might make tremendous headway. Other days you may struggle to complete one small task. It's all good -- as long as you are moving forward.

One final word of advice on procrastination: If you've tried every tip and despite your very best efforts, you continue to stall on a particular thing, move on. Let it go. That project or goal is probably just not appropriate for you right now.

Don't let one stalled desire upset your whole life balance. Keep moving ahead in other areas. Letting go of something often opens up a world of new possibilities.

The key to dealing with procrastination is to keep in mind that forward motion is what matters.

Live on Your Own Terms

You can't live a big, bold life on someone else's terms.

If you're like many people, you've unwittingly adopted other people's metrics of success as your own. This happens by osmosis. People usually conform to their parents' or society's opinions of what's important.

But to have a life you passionately love, you need to question whose rules you're playing by. You need to ask yourself what success actually means to you.

This is where courage comes into the equation.

Maybe your parents, teachers and mentors all valued academic achievement and you're haunted by the notion that you should get a master's degree. But deep in your heart, you're passionate about entrepreneurship and nothing would excite you more than to launch a small business.

What direction do you go? Do you make the choice to live up to other people's hopes and dreams for you? Or do you kick external approval to the curb and do your own thing?

I've seen far too many waste years living for the approval of other people. They are usually fully unaware they're doing it. Many have wildly impressive resumes, but their bliss level is on empty.

The question is: How full is your bliss tank?

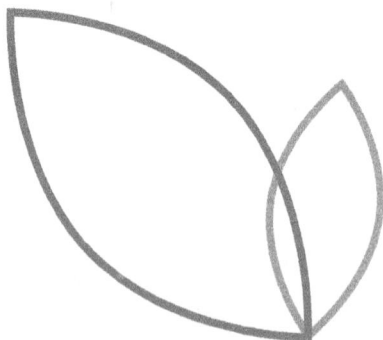

Read the following statements and ask yourself if any represent your beliefs. Be brutally honest with yourself.

1 When I'm considering a major life change, I think about how I'm going to explain it to my partner, parents, mentors or friends.

2 I rarely make any life choice that would disappoint my partner or parents.

3 If family or friends question a decision I'm making, it must be wrong.

4 It's important to me that family and friends are impressed by my life choices.

5 It would make me uncomfortable to create a life that was wildly different from the lives of my family and friends.

If any of these ring true for you, it's likely that you're weighing other people's opinion of you heavily into your life choices. Don't sell yourself or others short. If you want a bigger life, you'll need to start making decisions that align with that little voice inside you, not the external chorus.

Readiness

LEADING QUESTION

What fear is most impeding my bliss?

Capacity

Capacity is your ability to cope with and manage all aspects of your life. It's both an art and a science.

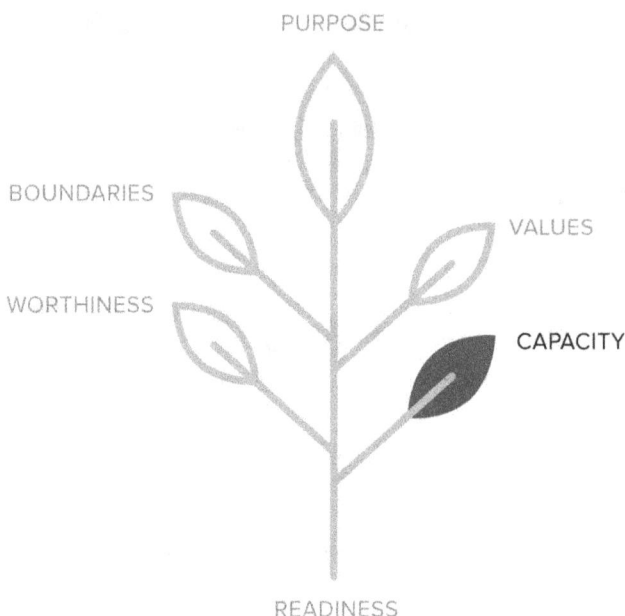

If you're living at **optimal capacity**, you easily manage your relationships, workload, fitness, emotions and spiritual health. If something unexpected gets thrown at you, you adapt quickly without much stress.

But if you're like most people, you're functioning 'under capacity' or 'above capacity.'

If you're **under capacity**, you spend a lot of time on stuff that isn't high priority to you. These things aren't leading you to the life you want.

When the day ends, you're often frustrated that so few things on your to-do list are done. You might be busy, but you're not highly productive.

If you're **above capacity,** you feel like your life is in fifth gear. The term 'wired' might apply to you. You often feel like you're doing a million things simultaneously. Moments of quiet reflection are rare. You are always 'on.' Sure, you're productive but you're on the verge of burnout. You're operating at a pace that's not healthy or sustainable.

To get into your optimal zone, you need to understand the 7 Elements of Capacity:

1 **Worthiness:** Love who you are.

2 **Psychological Well-Being:** See the bigger picture, handle whatever comes your way.

3 **Physical Self-Care:** Take care of your body.

4 **Relational Vitality:** Be deeply connected to the people you love, feeling part of a community.

5 **Personal Growth:** Feel energized about your life and where you're going.

6 **Environmental Management:** Have a sense of control of your surroundings.

7 **Self-Mastery:** Lead a balanced, flowing life. Easily managing new things that come along.

About the 7 Elements of Capacity

The pyramid below illustrates how the **7 Elements of Capacity** build on each other, creating your capacity to **live big.**

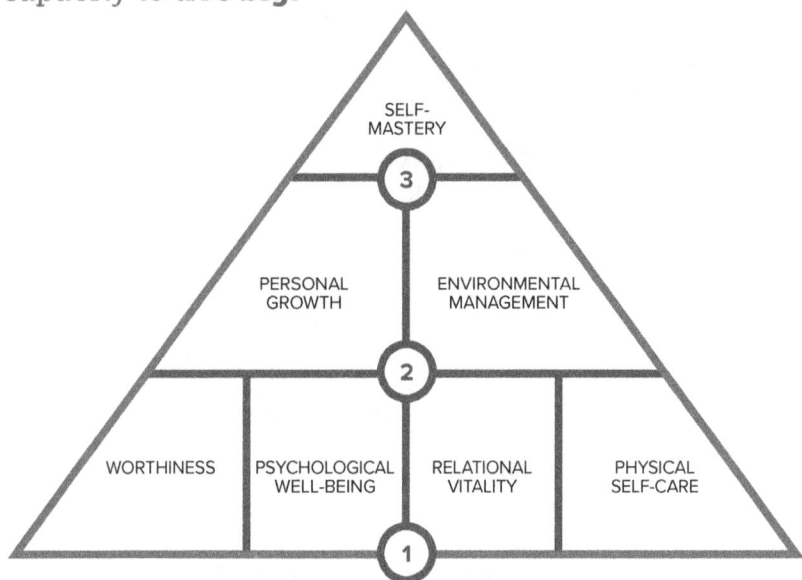

LEVEL 1 Basics: Without these basic elements of personal wellness in place, it's not possible to be at optimal capacity. You're running on empty if you don't have these covered.

LEVEL 2 Build: With the basics of personal wellness in place, you're now in a position to be in charge of your circumstances and to focus on personal growth.

LEVEL 3 Bonus: Once you're in charge of your circumstances and you've got a clear road map for personal growth, you're ready to have a balanced, flowing life. You're able to take on whatever life hands you.

"Don't underestimate the value of doing nothing, of just going along, listening to all the things you can't hear, and not bothering."

Pooh's Little Instruction Book,
inspired by A.A. Milne

Start a Rejuvenation Program

Everyone needs time and space for rejuvenation and personal growth. This is common sense. So, why do so many people neglect to take the time?

Lack of capacity is the biggest reason. It stems from a belief that the world, as you know it, will end if you take time for rest and reflection. Projects will come to a screeching halt, colleagues will wander aimless and confused through your office corridors, family and friends will freak out en masse.

It's helpful to let go of the idea that giving yourself time to rejuvenate is somehow a disservice to society. This is a myth that has led many people to the dark, dismal corner of the universe known as burnout. Do not follow in their footsteps.

You're human. You need breathing room to pursue new thinking, process information and make needed changes in yourself. If it takes every ounce of your energy to just get through the day, you'll never find breathing room. You'll never evolve.

The biggest piece of advice I can offer is simply to schedule in rejuvenation time. I mean that literally. Pull up your calendar and schedule in time for workouts, walks in nature, journaling, spa days, weekend getaways, meditation, hiking ... whatever restores you.

I have a client who scheduled monthly massages on her calendar and another who allotted weekly playground time with his son.

Inevitably, I see the same results again and again. When people make downtime a true priority, their stress level visibly drops. Their sense of ease comes back, along with their sense of humor.

Next thing you know, they're making decisions more swiftly. Tensions ease at home and work.

Treat your rejuvenation program with the same importance you give other commitments. If you don't take it seriously and you constantly postpone these vital activities, your capacity for life will suffer.

If your rejuvenation program is really humming, your capacity for life will expand. You'll be more clear-headed, productive and energized.

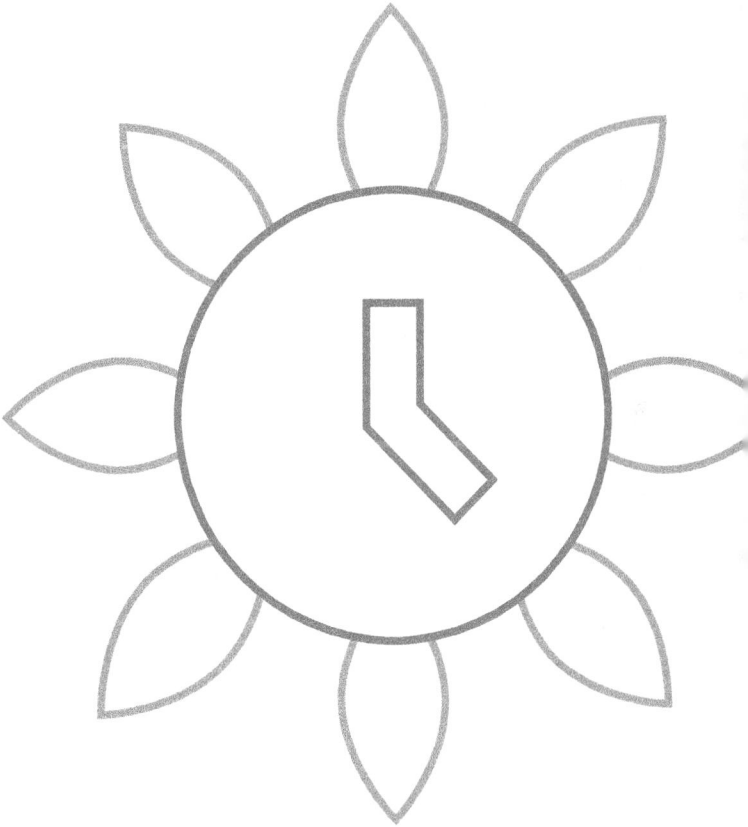

That Nagging Feeling: *'I want to do more with my life'*

Is there a chance that you're living beneath your true capacity?

There's no disgrace in that. I see talented, driven people all the time in this situation.

It doesn't mean you're lazy or unambitious. It doesn't mean you're not successful. So, let's take those notions right off the table.

Being under capacity means that you'd like to be doing more with your life, but something is getting in the way. Most likely, *you're* getting in your way and you don't even know it.

Often when people feel a sense of aimlessness about their lives, or a sense of exasperation at not knowing what their true purpose is, these are clues that they have untapped capacity.

This is a problem that's usually undiagnosed. I've seen people live this way for decades before understanding why they're so frustrated or listless. It can be debilitating.

Discovering that you're living beneath your full capacity is a fabulous thing, if you allow it to be.

It means that your life is about to open up. It means that, if you're brave enough to go on a journey of self-discovery and embrace change, anything is possible.

So, be real with yourself. Here are 7 statements to consider. How many of these feel true for you?

1 I see opportunities all around me but I don't often act on them.

2 I spend time with whoever wants to spend time with me.

3 I would like to feel a deeper sense of community.

4 I feel stuck.

5 I'd like to develop new attitudes and behaviors.

6 I'd like to be different in the future.

7 A lot of my time is unfocused.

If 4 or more of these statements feel true for you, you are likely living below your true capacity. It's high time to start a journey to discover what will make you fully thrive.

Life: How Much Can You Handle?

Your ability to handle life is entirely about balancing action and rest. It's as simple as asking, how well are you taking care of yourself?

Read the following statements. How many are true for you:

1 I spend time with the people who are important to me and whose company I enjoy.

2 I give myself the same love and attention I give to others.

3 I exercise regularly and eat healthy meals.

4 I feel rejuvenated when I wake up in the morning.

5 I can bounce back from almost anything.

6 When a curve ball comes my way, I respond calmly and without anger.

7 Outside of my work, my life has meaning.

If 6 or 7 of these statements feel very true for you, well done. You're operating at (or very close to) your optimal capacity. Find ways to stay in this zone.

If 5 or fewer of these statements feel very true for you, it's time to examine how you are balancing action with replenishment. You are either 'above' or 'under' your ideal capacity.

Stop Pushing Yourself to the Brink

It's a sad truth that we live in a society that glamorizes stress. If you're insanely busy, it must mean you're important, talented and in demand. Right?

No. Just no.

If you're insanely busy as a manner of course, bad things will transpire. Your body will break down, your mind won't function well, you'll discover your emotional breakpoint.

Working yourself to the bone can lead to depression, insomnia and a host of other serious health problems.

And what's it all for? It's based on a false assumption that you're more valuable to society, your family and your employer if you sustain the busiest, craziest pace you possibly can.

I can't tell you how many times I've seen this destructive behavior – literally too many times to count. And every time I say the same thing, 'You at your busiest is not the same as you at your best.'

Busy doesn't equal excellent. It doesn't equal fulfillment, satisfaction or optimal achievement.

Pushing yourself to the brink will spell disaster at home, work and everywhere else you find yourself. So stop kidding yourself. Start honoring your body, mind and spirit. You may be shocked to discover you actually get more done, and that you can operate at a higher caliber.

Your mission is to buck the cultural norm. Stop promoting stress as a way of life. Be an example of healthy, sustainable productivity.

Capacity

LEADING QUESTION

What's stopping me from operating at optimal capacity?

Worthiness

I feel that some people glaze over when they hear the term **worthiness**. Maybe it's overused. Maybe people feel helpless at the hugeness of it.

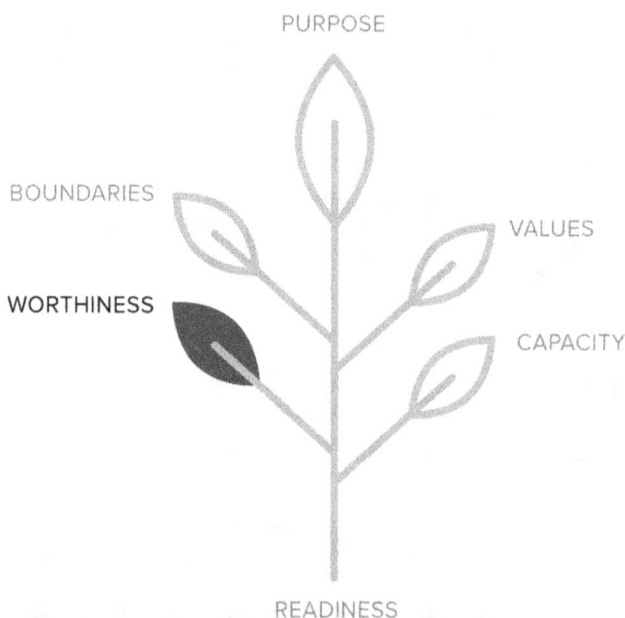

PURPOSE

BOUNDARIES

VALUES

WORTHINESS

CAPACITY

READINESS

I want to try to make it real for you because the truth is that your level of **worthiness** is, to a very large degree, dictating your life. This is not an over-statement.

Self-worth isn't some vague, esoteric thing. You can assess it. You can find the root causes of it. And please hear this: You can increase it.

I've seen achievers of the highest order. Some are satisfied with their lives and some struggle to find any meaning at all. The variance usually comes down to self-worth.

So let's get to it. What really is **worthiness**?

It's feeling that you deserve good things in life. It's an absence of feeling guilty, or like an imposter in your own skin. It's truly loving who you are, just as you are, regardless of what your job is. Regardless of how others see you. Regardless of whether you achieve anything at all, ever again.

Let me get a bit academic for just a moment. Worthiness is comprised of two things: self-concept (the thoughts you have about yourself) and self-esteem (how you feel about yourself).

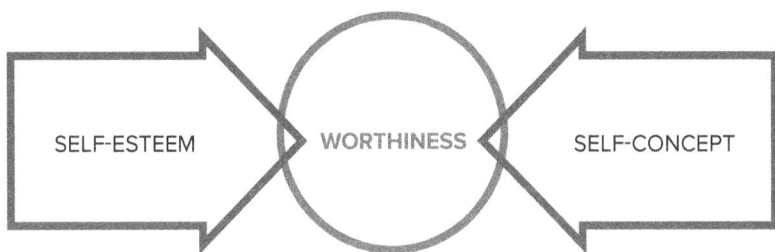

```
SELF-ESTEEM  >  WORTHINESS  <  SELF-CONCEPT
```

It's entirely possible to think all kinds of fabulous things about yourself (e.g., I'm amazing at tennis. I'm a phenomenal manager. My parenting skills rock.), but feel bad about yourself a lot of the time. If so, you have high self-concept and low self-esteem.

Some people beat themselves up constantly with negative thoughts. Usually they're barely aware they're doing it.

Their internal voice natters away with comments like, 'I can't believe you just said that,' 'You're the worst manager in the company,' and 'You don't deserve a happy family life.'

This type of thinking is often accompanied by negative feelings about yourself. Someone like this has low self-concept and low-self esteem, creating low self-worth.

If you have low **worthiness**, you don't feel grounded or safe in your own skin. You feel like anything good if your life could disappear at a moment's notice. You are inherently limited from having everything you want because deep down you feel you don't deserve it.

On the other hand, you have high self-worth when your internal voice sings your praises and you mostly feel pretty darn fantastic about yourself. You feel worthy regardless of the circumstances that may surround you at any given moment.

No matter how strong your **worthiness** *already is, you can increase it. Please – do so. Your possibilities in life expand with every ounce of self-worth you gain. There's no such thing as too much.*

"When you get to
a place where you
understand that
love and belonging,
your worthiness, is
a birthright and not
something you have
to earn, anything
is possible."

Brené Brown

Get to Know Your Worthiness

Let's talk about your level of worthiness, shall we? Sounds a little intimidating, I know. Don't panic.

It's totally okay to acknowledge areas of deficiency in your self-worth. Anyone who is on a path of personal growth must do this. It's the only way to move beyond your limitations.

The statements below indicate high worthiness. How true is each statement for you?

1 I feel that I truly deserve everything I have in my life.

2 I feel at any moment that something amazing might happen for me.

3 If I take away all of the roles I play in my life, I still love who I am at the very core. If those roles were to go away, I would still love myself deeply.

4 I have a clear understanding of who I am outside of my job, my hobbies and my relationships.

5 When negative things happen in my life, I don't see them as punishment.

6 I am kind to myself.

7 I treat myself with the same respect and appreciation that I give to others.

You may have just uncovered some new insight into your self-worth. No matter how worthy you feel, you can always feel more.

So, here are 3 ways to boost your worthiness:

1 **Spend time with positive people in positive places.** Don't let negative people or situations define who you are, or drain your energy. Notice who you spend the most time with and where you spend the most time. Would you describe these as positive, energizing people and places?

2 **Let praise and criticism roll off your back.** Don't let praise or criticism impact your self-worth. If you're dependent on what other people think, you'll never be at ease. Whose criticism are you most fearful of? Whose praise do you most desire? Just let go of both. Let go of caring what anyone else thinks.

3 **Get comfortable with being uncomfortable.** If you want to grow, you'll need to stretch your limits. You'll need to try new things and take measured risks. Be forewarned: this will be uncomfortable at times. Go with the discomfort. It's a sign you're shifting. Be willing to accept both success and failure as you try new things. You're learning and growing either way.

Remember the path to a bigger, bolder life is paved with worthiness.

How Joy Unveiled My Dark Little Secret

Sometimes self-worth issues show up in surprising ways. That happened for me recently when I was thinking about joy.

In her book *Daring Greatly*, Brené Brown (of TED Talk fame), says joy is one of the most difficult emotions to feel and sustain. This caught me off guard because I thought, 'That can't be right … don't I often feel joy?'

But I realized something alarming. What I often feel is what she calls 'foreboding joy.' Be on high alert – she says it's pervasive in our society.

Foreboding joy is a niggling feeling that even when everything appears to be going deliriously well, you feel at any moment something could go terribly wrong.

Does this ring a bell?

When I read this concept, a flood of memories from every stage of my life came back. I realized that for me joy is often paired with fear.

I vividly recall the joy of watching my newborn son in his crib fused with the terror of something bad happening to him. And the excitement of landing a lucrative project and the simultaneous anxiety I might somehow lose it.

As a teen, I felt sheer freedom when my parents went out for the night, leaving me in charge. Yet still I fretted they would have a car accident and not make it home.

Brown says people who live with the unconscious idea that joy leads to disaster believe they're just not worthy of joy.

This struck me like a thunderbolt: I don't fully believe I'm worthy of joy, even though I consider my life quite joyful.

And that's the moment I realized my own self-worth problem. Joy makes you feel vulnerable. If you don't feel worthy of it, it makes you feel like you have everything to lose.

At least I know I'm not alone. Brown believes as a culture we are 'joy-starved' because we're always seeking the next thing (product, relationship, job, etc.) that will bring us happiness.

She says we're a culture of scarcity even though we have abundance all around us. We're always reaching for something more than we've already got. We're always afraid to lose what we have.

I know from my own personal experience and through my work as a leadership coach, self-worth can be improved. It can be continually deepened and expanded.

I also know that even if you're many years along on your path of personal development, there's still work to be done. There are aspects of your self-identity still waiting to be discovered.

That's what happened to me. Thank you, Brené Brown.

The Irony of Worthiness

Some of us grow up with the really unfortunate belief that it actually matters what others think of us. And, worse yet, that how others see us is somehow indicative of who we really are.

Now let me be clear: I'm not advocating antisocial or uncompassionate behavior. Far from it. I'm simply saying that if you live your life with the primary goal of getting external validation, you're going to chase a lot of dreams that aren't really yours.

Scary but true, this happens subconsciously. If you're thinking, 'I don't do that ... I'm entirely my own person,' I encourage you to look really deeply and notice your thought patterns. Notice if you do certain things because you feel that's what someone else would expect of you and to keep up with the Joneses.

I feel that the real meaning of worthiness is starting to break into mass consciousness with the current anti-bullying trend and campaigns like, 'It Gets Better.' These campaigns are asking kids not to buy into the idea that the way others see them is reality.

Adults that witness childhood bullying can usually see with stark clarity that the bullies (the external world) are seeing the individual (the bullied child) with a tainted view. You want to embrace that vulnerable child and say, 'It's just not true. Please don't let others tell you who you are.'

The adult version of this scenario is often far, far more subtle. Typically the external world isn't bullying you (although maybe it is). More often, it's telling you things like, 'You'll be happier if you lobby for that big promotion,' 'People will think more highly of you if you live in a gorgeous house' and 'You're only a great parent if your child is at the top of the class.'

Consciously, you may not buy into any of that stuff. But with so much programming from society that self-worth comes from external sources, it's hard not to be persuaded.

see many people who are unaware that their anxiousness or dissatisfaction with life stems mostly from basing their worth on societal ideals rather than focusing on loving who they already are. You can actually achieve rather a lot by focusing on external validation, but in my experience, you'll never feel whole and thriving.

To me, the irony of self-worth is that it's possible to spend your entire lifetime worrying about what others think of you when the truth is, others aren't thinking of you that much at all. They're thinking of themselves, worrying what you think of them.

A Lesson from Oprah

If you felt no fear at all, how would you live your life? Would it be radically different from the way you live now?

People have all kinds of reasons for not living out their true desires, but at the end of the day, it mostly comes down to fear. It's fear of failure, fear of embarrassment, fear of disappointment, fear of rejection … fear of actually getting what you want. Fear of losing what you already have.

I help people see the fears that impede their lives. And although it may be uncomfortable to hear this, the fear is usually rooted in feelings of worthlessness.

That's why Oprah is so fascinating to me. Her early life (poverty, abandonment, molestation, teen pregnancy) could easily have burdened her with feelings of fear and worthlessness for a lifetime.

But somehow she found the tenacity to make life decisions based on her true desires and true capacity. Her self-worth seems to be at the highest end of the spectrum.

This doesn't mean we should all aspire to Oprah's life. It just means that if you've ever questioned whether your fears and self-worth are hard-coded into your DNA, Oprah is living proof they're not.

So is low worthiness tethering you? Maybe you've stayed at the same company or in the same industry because it seems like the only option. Maybe fear limits your ability to innovate or to step into more responsible roles. Maybe it stops you from creating a harmonious, loving family life.

If the elements of your life would be significantly different were it not for fear and hesitation, it's time to work on your self-worth.

"The thing you fear
most has no power.
Your fear of it is
what has the power.
Facing the truth will
set you free."

Oprah Winfrey

Worthiness

LEADING QUESTION

What self-limiting belief is trampling on my dreams?

Values

We are about to zero in on your core **values**.
Hang onto your hat. This one is a game-changer.

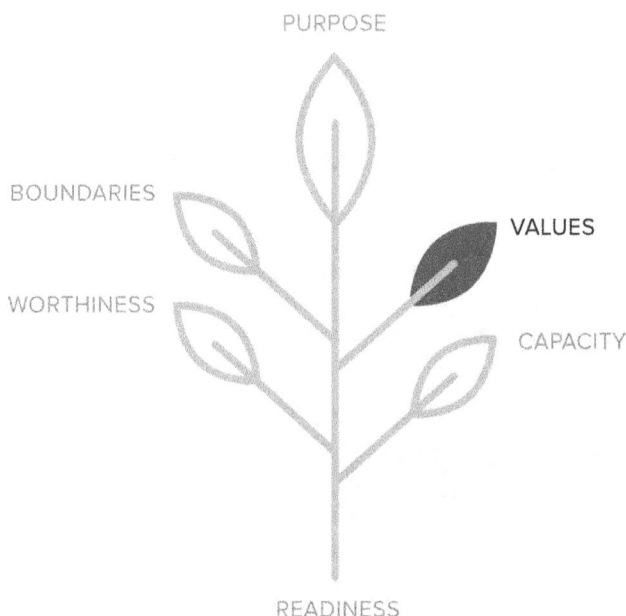

PURPOSE

BOUNDARIES

WORTHINESS

VALUES

CAPACITY

READINESS

Your core **values** are the principles that matter most to you. They reflect your highest priorities and most deeply held beliefs. They are like the GPS of your soul, directing your life toward your unique happiness (if you follow them).

Red alert: it is entirely impossible to live a bigger, bolder life unless your decisions are aligned with your core values.

When you allow them to guide your personal and career choices, your experience of life changes for the better.

You'll feel strong and purposeful, connected to your life's unique meaning. You won't struggle with questions about who you are and what you're meant to do.

It's easy to be true to you and to make smart decisions. You don't find yourself worrying about whether you're doing the right thing.

When you're living according to your core **values,** you are living an authentic life. You're the real you.

And this, my friend, is a giant source of happiness.

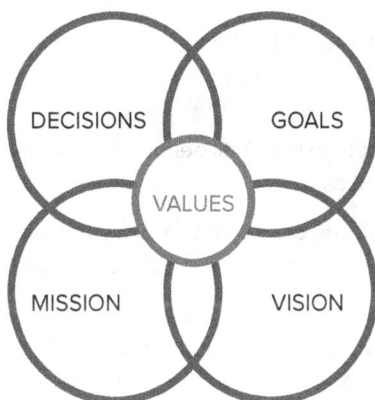

When you know your core **values,** everything else can fall into place: your life vision, mission and goals. Decision-making becomes dead easy.

It's possible your life is out of sync with your core values and you don't even know it.

Maybe you've never considered them, or you have only a vague sense of what they are. Or maybe you've accidentally focused on values that aren't truly core to you (but are core to people close to you like family, friends or colleagues).

If so, you may have a nagging, indefinable sensation that something is missing. Or a subtle discomfort now and again, like something is wrong but you don't know what it is.

Or you might find yourself continually getting into unpleasant situations and wondering how in the world you ended up there. Again.

Don't let yourself be seduced by other people's core values, however lovely they may be. Living someone else's values will never lead to your bliss.

Take the time to unearth your core **values.** Then take the bold step of living your life according to them. This is fundamental to living a bigger, more meaningful life.

The Emptiness of Goals Without Values

Here's a wild thought: Traditional goal setting is the enemy of bliss.

I'll tell you why. The goal setting we've all been taught is absent of the most vital aspect of your life: your values.

Sure, if you hack away at it, you can set any random goal and achieve it if you want to. Maybe you'll enjoy an initial jolt of satisfaction, but sustainable bliss will elude you.

This is the reason so many talented, accomplished people are searching to fill a void they don't understand. They're achieving, but their not syncing their life to some grander plan. They lack a sense of meaning.

Before you select your next big endeavor or create a new set of resolution ... stop. Breathe. Take the time to look inward. Understand what matters most to you. Figure out the kind of person you want to be in this world.

When you've nailed that down, you'll be ready to articulate life goals that lead you in the right direction. You'll likely feel a stronger motivation to doggedly pursue these goals, unlike random resolutions that are too often forgotten a few weeks on.

Goals aligned to your core values will have far deeper meaning for you when you achieve them. You will feel a lasting, deep-down-in-your-soul satisfaction that past achievements lacked.

And so yes, be bold. If you want a bigger, more fulfilling life, start setting goals that make your soul soar.

Change the Game

I know from personal experience that living by your values changes the game.

Years ago when I was the owner of a booming PR agency, I was faced with one of the biggest decisions of my life. Two impressive companies made bids to acquire my business.

At the time, I was counseled to make my decision based on the most lucrative offer and you may be thinking to yourself, 'No brainer. Always go with the highest bidder.'

But knowing what I know now, I would have used different criteria. I would have asked myself which option most closely fit my core values.

And guess what? If I had, it's likely I wouldn't have sold the business at all. Now I know one of my core values is 'freedom.' I had far more freedom as an independent business owner than a partner in a large firm. I was successful there, but never happy.

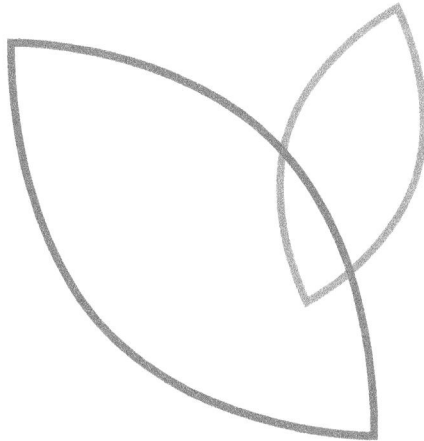

Find Your Core Values

Your core values are not an abstract notion. They should be a precise, succinct list of words you can rattle off at the drop of a hat.

They are the principles you value above all others in your personal and professional life.

It's crucial that you have an emotional connection to each one. They should make you feel energized, purposeful and clear.

When you live by your values, you'll make decisions and create plans that excite you. You'll lead your life in a way that's more genuine. People will respond to you differently.

Here's a framework to discover and live by your core values:

1 **Find the words.** Get your mind away from stress and the details of life. Sit in a park on the grass with your iPad or journal, and let your mind roam free. What do you value? Start writing whatever springs to mind.

Play with words like passion, discovery, adventure, contribution, creativity and freedom (to name just a few).

DO NOT ANALYZE. Analyzing will send you down the wrong path. Let this exercise be quick and painless. Just notice which words make your heart sing. Choose 4 that make it sing the loudest. Done!

2 **Make them central to your life.** Start with simple things like posting them on your fridge or making them the background image on your computer. You need to see them constantly.

As the stuff of life arises, requiring personal and business decisions, use your values as a filter. Ask yourself what decision will be most aligned with them. Trust yourself and your values. They will steer you in a direction of integrity and truth.

3 **Be authentic.** For example, if you choose 'adventure' as a core value, but you live a very conventional life and make only prudent, conservative decisions ... you aren't living by that core value.

I'm not saying you need to be crazy and reckless. I'm just saying you need to live from a place that's authentic to who you are.

Gut Check: Are You Being the Real You?

I never tire of seeing people become reinvigorated by their lives when I help them tune into and articulate their core values. It's like an inner light bulb turns on, illuminating their true essence.

But knowing your values and living them are 2 different things.

Living them requires breaking old habits and being comfortable with making decisions that might unsettle other people.

If you're an established lawyer who's just realized, for example, that beauty is a core value, you might alarm people if you start pursuing your secret passion for architecture.

To onlookers, that kind of realignment might seem rash. But it's not. You gotta be you.

Having said this, living your values doesn't necessarily require dramatic upheaval. It's mostly about the subtle aspects of how you live.

Let me help you get a gut check on how well you're currently living your values.

Select one of your core values and ask yourself:

1 Do I exude this value in the way I speak?

2 Do I exude this value in the way I present myself to the world?

3 Do I exude this value in my career choices?

4 Do I exude this value in the way I spend my free time?

5 Is this value evident in my leadership style?

Repeat this process for your other core values (maximum 4).

Values

LEADING QUESTION

What parts of my life are not aligned to my values?

Boundaries

Let's start here: A huge percentage of life's everyday stress and anxiety comes from having a lack of **boundaries**.

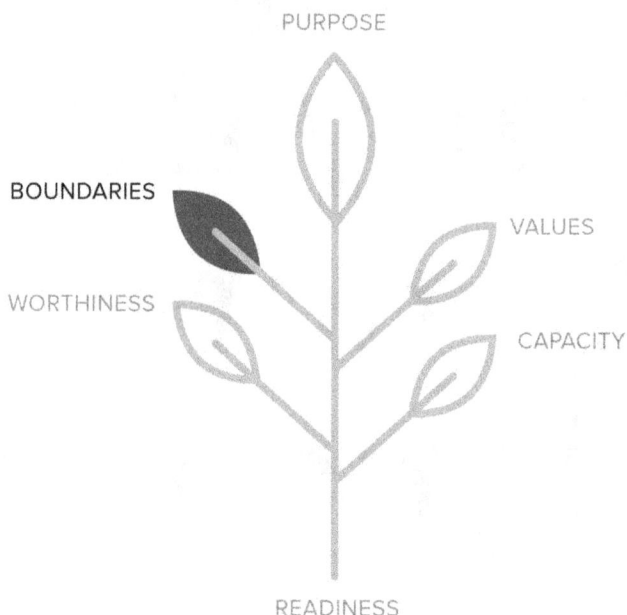

PURPOSE

BOUNDARIES

VALUES

WORTHINESS

CAPACITY

READINESS

Boundaries are the personal laws that guide how you want to behave in the world and how you want to be treated.

Your **boundaries** act like an invisible barrier that surrounds you, marking your personal space. The outside world doesn't know they're there unless you communicate your boundaries.

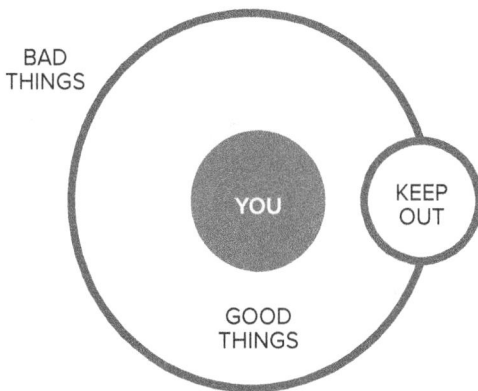

But if you're like most people, you don't actively set your personal **boundaries.** This leads you to do things you regret sometimes. You may feel frustrated and infuriated by the way some people treat you.

If you lack personal boundaries, every relationship will be affected. At home, you may feel disrespected by kids who speak to you in that tone that works your last nerve. Or a spouse who continually makes social plans without consulting you or always disrupts your quiet moments of peace.

At work you may find people talking over you in meetings, switching game plans without asking you, or assuming you'll work into the wee hours of the night.

At first, these things may feel like minor annoyances. But over time, as your personal **boundaries** are continually invaded, your ability to cope wears down. Then things can get ugly. Annoyance turns to fury.

Maybe you have a sudden burst of irrational rage at a driver that cuts you off. Or you scream ferociously at your 5-year-old for chattering non-stop or at your spouse for forgetting a commitment. At work, you may make snide comments about your colleagues, or respond to requests with barely suppressed hostility.

None of this is conducive to a big, blissful life.

So get crystal-clear about your personal boundaries.
And be unafraid to communicate them.

Whose Boundaries Are You Crossing?

I'm going to ask you to consider an uncomfortable question: Are you unknowingly crossing other people's personal boundaries?

Don't answer 'no' quite so quickly.

The fascinating (and terrifying) thing about personal boundaries is that they are unique to each individual. Maybe you grew up in a household where it was totally acceptable to sample the food off someone else's plate, interrupt when someone was speaking or use sarcasm to get a quick laugh.

Now you're out in the world. Maybe you're managing a team, raising children and interacting with people from all walks of life. Unbeknownst to you, certain social habits you consider entirely ordinary could be (silently) freaking people out.

People aren't likely to tell you when you're crossing a boundary. So, you need to become a keen observer of yourself and others.

The first step is to notice your social habits. Be honest with yourself – do you cut people off if you have something to say? Do you speak louder than necessary? Could your humor be considered off-putting? Do you press people for commitments before they're ready?

Start with your next interaction. Try tuning in more carefully to how people respond to you and how they're feeling about their interaction with you.

Recently, I hosted a leadership workshop for 30 managers at a telecom company. During a discussion on boundaries, lightning struck for one of the participants.

He thought about a management tactic he'd been using forever: wandering through the halls popping in unexpectedly to visit his employees. His habit was to walk into people's offices, lean over their desks and check up on their activities.

His intention was to keep a steady flow of communication and contact. The reality was, he was being disrespectful.

Self-awareness is the only path to respecting other people's personal boundaries. You don't need to be paranoid or self-conscious. Just allow yourself to get out of your own head and become more aware of what's happening around you.

You'll learn a lot about yourself, and you're likely to find that people are more open with you than ever before.

Avoiding Rage at Home and Work

Have you ever watched someone become completely unglued because they were cut off in traffic? Or because a server got a food order wrong or a clerk couldn't process a refund.

You've seen that person, right? They're a freaking out, spitting fire, a temporary whirling dervish of rage.

Have you ever been that person?

Moments of irrational fury are not something anyone cares to experience, but it's happened to the best of us. You may have wondered if it's just human nature to burst at the seams on occasion, or if the demands of a busy life are wearing you thin.

My view is that this kind of rage often has a common origin. It comes from not setting clear boundaries for yourself at work and in life.

Over time, these infringements on your personal space wear you thin, and frustration about how you're treated at home and work starts to build into fury. And fury has a nasty habit of erupting at the most inappropriate and unexpected times.

If you want to avoid unpredictable rage, you need to consider how well you are setting boundaries.

Here are 5 boundary questions to ask yourself:

1 At work, do others listen politely when you speak or do you have to fight to be heard?

2 At work, do you feel your co-workers respect your time? Or do you find yourself working more hours than others or assuming other people's responsibilities?

3 At home, do people speak to you in a manner and tone you consider polite?

4 At home, have you been clear with others about how much personal time you need?

5 At work and at home, if you are starting to feel overwhelmed, do you ask for help?

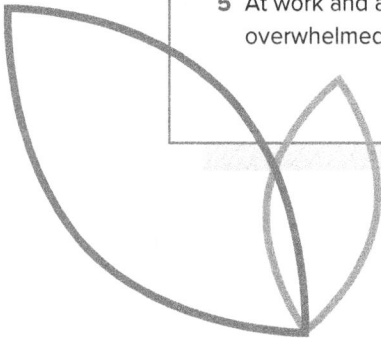

If you answered, yes to all of these ... well done. You know how to set boundaries. If you answered 'no' to any of these, heads up. Boundaries are key to a calmer life. They are an antidote to fury.

You Need Boundaries Too

Something they don't always teach in school is that the road to respect is paved with boundaries.

In this case, I'm talking about boundaries that protect you from the behaviors of those around you. Think of them as rules that limit how others may interact with you.

Think of your personal boundaries as an invisible circle around you that helps you keep the good things in and the bad things out.

Your personal boundaries already exist for you but they're likely unconscious, meaning you haven't actually articulated them to yourself.

Unarticulated boundaries are a mighty dangerous territory, especially for anyone seeking to live a bigger, bolder life. They are breached far too often.

If you want to create bliss and harmony, you need boundaries that are perfectly, undeniably clear to you. Because when they are clear to you, then you can communicate them to others.

One way to identify your personal boundaries is to notice when people are not treating you in a manner you like. You'll often experience an emotional response like frustration, sadness or anger when this happens.

When you feel this way, try to pinpoint the exact behavior that triggered your reaction, e.g., your colleague is late for a meeting again. Most likely, this means you have a boundary about punctuality.

Conversely, when you enjoy an interaction with someone else, pay attention to what behavior(s) you appreciate. This is often a clue as to how you'd like to interact with others.

Start to get clear on your personal rules right now. Write down your top 5 personal boundaries.

Here are some common personal boundaries, just to get your thoughts flowing.

1 I don't gossip about family, friends or colleagues.

2 I listen carefully when someone else is speaking, rather than thinking about how I will respond.

3 I am on time for appointments and end them promptly.

4 I speak to others in a respectful tone, even when I'm annoyed.

5 I am mindful that people have stresses outside of work that may influence their behavior.

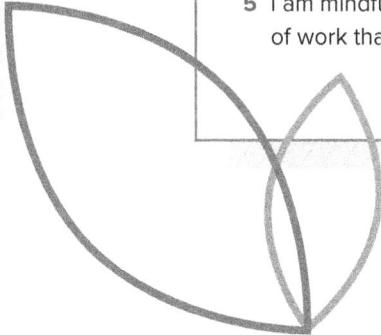

Once you've identified these personal rules as to how you want to behave in the world, you'll find it easy to set boundaries as to how you want to be treated.

Over time, consider expanding your list of personal rules. You will have many more unarticulated boundaries to draw on. Eventually you may have a list of rules for home, work, friends and community life.

I Broke My Own Rule

Recently I broke a rule I set for myself when I first became a parent. I yelled at my teenage son and believe me, it rocked us both.

I don't claim to be a perfect parent but my son is accustomed to me speaking to him in a calm, compassionate way. I make a point of it. It represents how I want to be as a parent, and how I want him to be in the world. Sure, I lose my patience and my tone changes. But yelling is forbidden.

So what happened? Why after years of being true to this personal boundary did I lose my cool and behave in a way I promised myself I never would?

I can chalk it up to a moment of overwhelm. I was in the midst of several major work projects, home renovations and the new challenges that come along with being the mom of a teen.

I can see the steps I could have taken to release some of the pressure I was feeling before it all erupted in a moment of exasperation. I could have given myself more time off, pushed some deadlines, or found some quiet time alone to decompress.

Yes, I could see where I went awry. The bigger question was: Could I forgive myself?

My first instinct was to beat myself up with self-blame. But then I realized this was a moment to show my son (and myself) what to do when you break your own rule.

So I apologized. I owned it. I recommitted to living up to the standard of behavior I believe in. I made some changes to release some of the pressure I was feeling. And, I forgave myself.

No one is perfect as a parent. No one is perfect in the business world. Perfection isn't my goal ... personal evolution is.

So, I learned about pushing myself too far and someone else paying the price. I learned about parenting with more humility. And I learned that even when you breach a personal boundary, you can move on with grace.

Boundaries

LEADING QUESTION

What personal rule do I break most often?

Purpose

Do you have a clear, resounding answer to the question, 'What's your **purpose** in life?'

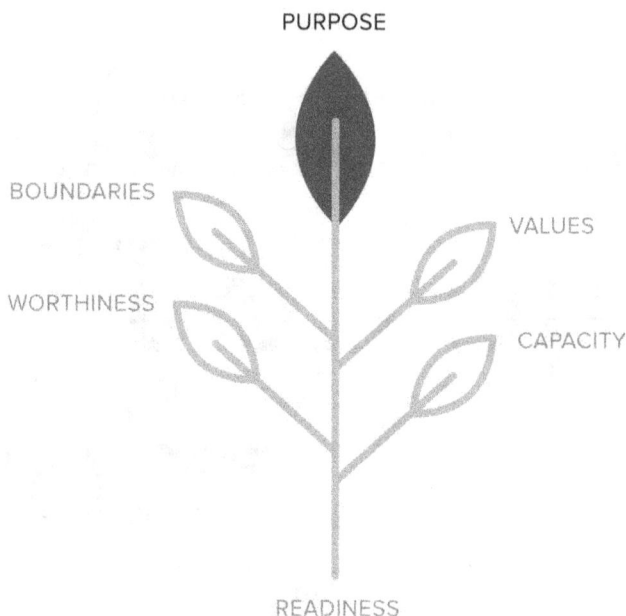

PURPOSE

BOUNDARIES

VALUES

WORTHINESS

CAPACITY

READINESS

Your **purpose** is the greater reason you do what you do. It is an enduring source of passion and commitment that drives the very big and very small things you do in life.

Being able to answer this question changes everything. It orients your life in the cosmos. Suddenly a job isn't just a job. Volunteering isn't just volunteering. Every act of being you is set on a grander stage, in a broader context.

If there are two great feats in life, surely one is to figure out your life's **purpose**. The other is to fulfill it.

YOUR PASSION — YOUR TALENT

PURPOSE

Being passionate about your life isn't something you can happily fake for long. In other words, if your marketing job is just about leads, or your accounting job is just about numbers, your passion will wane ... likely sooner than later.

If on the other hand you have tuned into a greater **purpose** for why you have chosen your life path and how your current situation aligns to that, you won't even have to try to be passionate. It will happen authentically.

For example, if you know that your **purpose** in life is to help people feel beautiful about themselves, your marketing job in the fashion industry takes on new life.

If you know your **purpose** is to help people turn their wild ideas into thriving businesses, your commitment to accounting is transformed. If you know you're on a mission to help eliminate homelessness, your community involvement is enlightened.

Having a clear sense of **purpose** matters because people around you sense it. Even if you're tremendously talented and crazy-productive, a lack of authentic passion is palpable to your colleagues, friends and family. There's a degree of trust that can only be attained when people sense your heart is really in it, and not having this will inhibit your ability to live big.

But this isn't just about other people and how they view you. Ultimately, it's about you living a life that you love and feeling connected to a **purpose** that actually matters to you.

This is foundational to feeling grounded and passionate about what you do. You can achieve a lot even if you don't have a **purpose**, but the accomplishments won't ever feel as meaningful or satisfying.

3 Revealing Questions

Right now, I'd like you to ask yourself 3 revealing questions:

1 Do you sometimes feel discomfort with your life and you can't trace the cause?

2 Do you sometimes question what you're here on this planet to do?

3 Do you feel you're quietly waiting for something to happen to make the pieces of your life fit together and make sense?

If you answered 'yes' to any or all of these questions, the fix may be closer than you think. Sure, these can be symptoms of an existential crisis, but they can also be symptoms of something more earthly ... a life out of sync with your purpose.

Let's begin here. We're living in a society that would have us believe everyone is made deliriously happy by achieving exactly the same things: money, white picket fence, luxury car, good job, 2.5 kids, 2 week vacations in Maui and eternal beauty.

There's nothing wrong with any of these things. But if you're focusing your life (consciously or not) on having them, it's worth pausing to ask yourself – are these things bringing you the wholeness you expected to feel?

If not, let's continue. That feeling of wholeness I'm referring to is what you feel when your life is aligned to a greater purpose. It's when you know why you spend your life doing what you do.

When you know your purpose and allow it to guide every personal and career decision you make, let me tell you, magic happens.

That icky, uncomfortable sense that something is wrong with your life but you don't know what it is, just goes away.

You know who you are. You know why you're here.

Find Your Purpose

You're the only person who can discover your greater reason for being. So I want you to ask yourself the following questions. Take your time with each one, but listen to your gut. Don't analyze or second-guess.

What does your inner voice say?

1 What specific aspects of your career (or vocation) do you find most fulfilling?

2 What aspects of your volunteer/community time do you find most fulfilling?

3 List 3 moments at work in the past year that you found truly meaningful.

4 What do the 3 moments from Question 3 all have in common?

5 When you think about the world we live in, what brings you discontent? If it were up to you, what would you fix about the world? Dr Martin Luther King, Jr. found his purpose in his discontent with civil rights. Steve Jobs was discontent that no one was making computer technology easily accessible to everyday people. What about you?

The insights you glean from these questions will be clues to your greater purpose. Don't worry if it isn't crystal-clear right away. It can take time to emerge. But if you're open and patient, the answer will arise.

Your Purpose is What You Deem It to Be

Let me help you avoid a deadly trap. As you hunt for your life purpose, don't get hung up on knowing your ultimate purpose right now and believing something is wrong with you if you can't find it. I've seen too many people get hung up on 'not knowing their purpose' and letting that keep them playing small.

Your purpose is what you name it. Pick something that feels reasonably right for the moment, and let yourself move forward. As you take action toward your current purpose, you'll learn. You'll understand yourself more deeply. As you do, you can clarify or even completely change your purpose.

What I'm saying is, don't let discovering your life's purpose be an excuse for inaction. Inaction won't get you closer to knowing your purpose. In fact, it's likely to keep you from ever discovering it.

Here's a quick exercise to get you started.

Now, without analyzing or over-thinking, write one sentence that answers the following question:

What are you here on this planet to do?

Go with your gut. Write from your heart and your intuition, not your mind.

Now observe. What have you written? Does it surprise you?

Remember, action begets inspiration. So now that you've named a purpose, start doing stuff to fulfill it. Now.

Living Your Purpose

Knowing your purpose and values is a lovely, heart-warming thing. But it won't change your life unless you do something about it and that's going to take courage.

You'll need to let extraneous distractions fall to the wayside and accept that some people might complain. They might want you to have different priorities. You need to be clear with yourself and others about where your time and focus will be invested.

You need to honor your commitments of course, so be acutely aware of the promises you're making.

It's been said a million times, but it's a fundamental truth: You can't be everything to everyone. Trying to be will never lead to a big, blissful life.

Your purpose and values are your North Star. They inform how you live your life as an individual, a parent, a spouse/partner, a colleague, a community member and any other roles you take on.

People with keen focus on their purpose and values are easy to spot. They are invigorated and inspiring. They're optimistic, exuberant forces of nature.

Your purpose and values will only change your life if you let them. You need to decide — will you treat them merely as intellectual concepts? Or will you live and breathe them every day.

This distinction will determine if you live small or live big.

As you begin to reorient your life, regularly check these statements as indicators of how well you're living up to your purpose and values:

1 My career choices are aligned to my purpose and values.

2 My volunteer/community work is aligned to my purpose and values.

3 My parenting style is aligned to my purpose and values.

4 The way I treat my partner/spouse is aligned to my purpose and values.

5 I make small and big decisions based on my purpose and values.

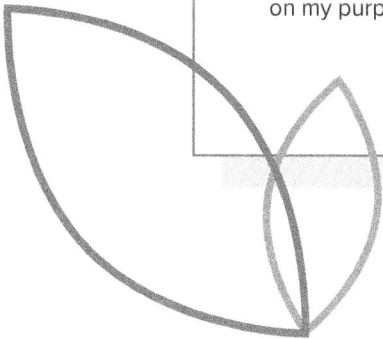

Purpose

LEADING QUESTION

If failure and fear ceased to exist, what would I do with my life?

Part Four:

ADVICE FOR
YOUR JOURNEY

Boldness Essentials

Your path to a bigger, bolder life has nothing to do with the external world and what it wants from you.

It has everything to do with secrets hidden deep inside you. Secrets about what you truly desire. Secrets about what you believe you deserve ... and don't deserve.

Most of these secrets are buried so deeply, they are completely invisible to you until you take decisive action to bring them to the surface.

This willingness to explore inward is perhaps the most courageous thing you will ever do in your life. It's the only way to create significant change. It's the only way to be your authentic self.

Without looking inward, you can't destroy the limiting beliefs that get in your way. You can't find your greatest happiness, even though you may have great achievements by other people's standards.

So be bold. Choose to find the real you. Be brave enough to live on your own terms, even if it means sometimes unsettling other people along the way. Even if it means being vulnerable and uncomfortable at times.

Believe me. It's worth it.

Here's what it takes to boldly explore inward:

1 Conviction

This is boldness to listen to yourself. Rather than following someone else's lead or comparing yourself to others, really listen to you. Don't buy into the idea that external validation means something. Be bold enough to validate yourself and your choices.

2 Perseverance

This is boldness to stay the course. Looking inward and living life on your own terms is definitely the most satisfying road, but it's not the easiest. You'll want to pack it in. It's hard to be open. Change is discomfort. Keep going. Believe in your ability to move through the difficult patches.

3 Curiosity

This is boldness to question everything. Don't be limited by old assumptions about yourself. Expand your mind wider than you thought possible. The possibilities for your life are endless, but to find them you need to go deep.

4 Risk-Taking

This is the boldness to leap. You can't live your biggest life without taking risks. You'll need to find resilience. There will be failures along the road – don't let them define you. Bounce back and make your next leap.

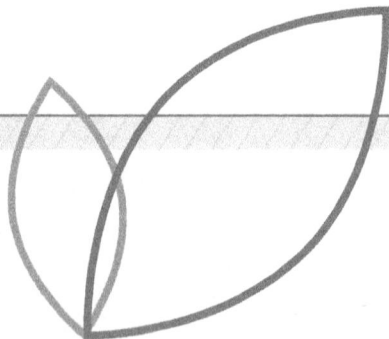

Don't Just Read it, Live it

Congratulations. You've just acquired insight into
6 practices that have the power to change your life.

But of course, insight alone will change very little.

Take Cassie, for example, from the intro to this book. She only found the strength to create a lifestyle she really loved when she honestly examined how she was holding herself back.

If Cassie was unwilling to look at her own behavior and beliefs, I can tell you with certainty she would still have a life of chaos and stress. She would still be searching for meaning.

That's why the 6 Live Bigger Practices need to be lived. They need to be used in your everyday work and life, guiding the choices you make and the way you engage in the world.

Used well, these practices will revolutionize how you see yourself and your potential. They will open your mind to bigger, bolder possibilities. They will shatter old behaviors and beliefs that stunt your happiness.

Make sure you keep fine-tuning each one in equal measure. They work as an integrated system.

Go beyond playing small and start living big.

Lisa

P.S. I love feedback. Please share your thoughts directly with me at:
lisa@lisamartininternational.com

Afterword

May I make a suggestion?

If you found this book of value, consider bringing the leadership development program, *LEAD + LIVE: 6 Practices to Live Bigger,* to your organization.

Just like this book, *LEAD + LIVE* helps leaders understand themselves at a deeper level so they can get out of their own way and live a values-based, purpose-driven life.

Program participants get past personal limitations, find genuine inspiration and tailor their career and life to their personal values and greatest strengths.

LEAD + LIVE is a flexible, turnkey licensing solution that comes with all the tools required to cultivate high-impact, thriving leaders.

In other words, you get a proven program with all the training materials you need, including online self-assessments, facilitator guides, workbooks, PowerPoint Decks, posters and, of course, this book.

And you have the freedom to deliver *LEAD + LIVE* your way on your schedule.

Acknowledgments

Thank you to the explorers and adventurers who have inspired me to live boldly. Most notably, I thank my parents who left Australia (and everyone they knew) in their mid-20's with 3-year-old me and my infant sister in tow. They left with the intention of living in Canada for two years and ended up staying a lifetime.

Their spirit of adventure and possibility shaped my worldview and gave me the confidence to go after my true desires. It's because of them that I'm not limited by fear.

Many writers and thinkers have influenced my desire and ability to keep thinking bigger about my own life and the way I counsel others, in particular Marshall Goldsmith, Brené Brown, Cheryl Richardson and Seth Godin.

And of course, thank you to my clients who are continually making big, brave leaps. I consistently learn from these tenacious individuals, who are willing to dig deep, stare fear down and create the lives they deserve.

Also, I honor all those daring individuals, present and past, who let their passion for exploration guide their lives – including Captain Cook, Amelia Earhart, Neil Armstrong, Dr. Roberta Bondar, Ben Saunders and Jessica Watson. Thank you for showing me how to live with a spirit of adventure.

And last, I thank all of you readers for taking the bold step of reading these pages. May your life be as big as you desire.

About the Author

Lisa Martin, PCC

Lisa Martin has made it her mission to help companies keep and cultivate leaders. She's the creator of the *Lead + Live Better*™ leadership programs; author of 5 books, including the bestselling *Briefcase Moms*; and a seasoned speaker, facilitator and executive coach.

For the past 15 years Lisa has designed and delivered leadership programs for PwC, TELUS, Vancouver Canucks, HSBC and UBC, to name a few.

Her powerful, easy-to-use *Lead + Live Better*™ turnkey leadership licensing solutions empower organizations to cultivate amazing leaders at every level.

She has coached thousands of people on the art of thriving as a leader and in life, and counseled companies on building leadership capacity.

As a speaker, Lisa is sought by international conferences, corporations and universities. She's known for her fun, straight-shooting speaking style and her intuitive sense for her audience.

She does all this as the founder of *Lisa Martin International*, a boutique leadership development firm with global scope, which equips organizations to deliver powerful leadership development in-house.

Lisa lives in North Vancouver with her husband, spirited teenaged son and two cats that act like toddlers.

You can find her at: **lisamartininternational.com**

"Be brave enough
to live on your own
terms. Trust me,
comfort won't lead
you anywhere new."

Lisa Martin

Cornerview Press
Box 30075
North Vancouver, BC
Canada V7H 2Y8

Edited by Jacqueline Voci
Cover and text design by Melissa Hicks & Melanie Iu
Cover image by Getty Images
Author Photo by Linda Mackie

ISBN 978-0-9734560-3-5

Library of Congress information is available on request.

The examples I've used in this book reflect the stories I've been privileged to share in my work as a leadership coach. To respect my clients' privacy, I have changed their names and other identifying details.

lisa MARTIN
LEAD+LIVE BETTER

Lisa's Lead+Live Better™ programs deliver advanced leadership and life skills in a fun, intuitive and straight-shooting way.

LEAD

6 Skills to Be a RockStar Leader

LEAD advanced

6 Skills to Be the Ultimate Executive

LEAD for women

Briefcase Moms

LEAD+LIVE

6 Practices to Live Bigger

LEAD+LIVE advanced

6 Practices to Master the Art of Thriving

lisamartininternational.com

www.ingramcontent.com/pod-product-compliance
Lightning Source LLC
Chambersburg PA
CBHW060323220326
41598CB00027B/4402